Prepper's Pantry

The Survival Guide To Modern Day Emergency Food & Water Storage

By Steve Plant

Contents

Introduction

Conclusion

Introduction

Your family is too important to ignore, right? You wouldn't ignore them and not go grocery shopping or prepare meals for them, would you? What if you lost your job or there was a major natural disaster? Would you just not feed them? Imagine the unthinkable, like a war or civil unrest that leaves the entire community or even country in a state of emergency. Feeding and caring for your family is still going to be a priority, but it is going to be much more difficult without the benefit of grocery stores, fast food restaurants, or even the help of the government.

You would be completely on your own. Your family would be depending on you to feed them, even if the world was in chaos. With the state of the world in such turmoil, the last thing you need on your plate is a starving family. It would turn you inside out to see your family suffer unnecessarily. Yes, it isn't necessary because you can do things today to ensure they do have full bellies and the nourishment they need to stay alive. You can ensure there is food to put on the table to keep your family going until things mellow out or you find a reliable resource of food.

By taking the time to start creating a prepper's pantry today, you can eliminate a great deal of stress and frustration should you ever find yourself in financial dire straits or facing an uncertain world. Nothing in this world is a guarantee. Just because you have a full pantry today and plenty of money in the bank to buy more food, it doesn't mean it will always be that way. Prepping is about preparing for an uncertain future. We never know what is around the next corner. Do what you can to make sure your children's bellies are full and you will not have to hear their cries for food.

Chapter 1

Planning Your Food Supply

Take a deep breath. There is no need to panic. Prepping is something you want to take in bite size bits and pieces. There is no point in taking on the monumental task of building up a long term food storage that will last your family a year all on the first day. Easing into it and setting reasonable goals is the way to go. This way you are still moving forward without getting overly stressed or trying to buy too much of any one thing and completely forgetting about another.

Planning your food supply should be approached with the mindset of starting with a short-term supply, about 3 months' worth of food, and building up to a medium-term supply of 6 months. Once you have crossed that threshold, you will aim for long-term, which is a year or more of food sitting in your prepper pantry.

It takes planning to build up adequate food storage. You can't just run to the grocery store and toss a bunch of stuff in the cart and then put it on your shelves and call it a day. Not only will that cost you a small fortune, it will likely not be a well-rounded pantry and you are going to be a bit hit and miss. You won't be able to prepare actual meals. It will be a can of chilli, a can of tuna and some crackers for dinner.

Short Term

A short term supply is about three months' worth of food on hand. The food can be a variety of canned, freeze-dried, dehydrated ingredients for preparing meals from scratch. Keep in mind; those nights of throwing a frozen pizza in the oven are going to be gone. Meal prep is going to take a little more effort. Think back to your grandma's time. She made everything right in her kitchen. She didn't have the option or luxury of a microwave to heat up a frozen dinner. It is all about cooking the old-fashioned way.

It would be next to impossible to find a list of food you should store fit to be perfect for your family. Your family isn't going to eat the same food as your neighbour and their family. Nor will your family require the same amount of food as the couple down the road who don't have children.

Jot down what you would typically serve the family in meals for one week. If you wrote in McDonald's or stopped at 7-11 for breakfast, you need to substitute those meals with something from your own kitchen.

Now take that list and identify and list out any ingredients you need to make every meal. Assume you will be serving that meal once a week for the next 12 weeks. Multiply each ingredient by 12 and you have your list of items you need to build up to a short term, 3-month food supply.

Let's go over some examples.

On Monday night you serve the family canned chilli with cornbread. You use two cans for the meal and one box of cornbread.

2x12=24 cans of chilli for 3 months assuming you eat chilli for dinner once a week.

1x12=12 boxes of cornbread. Now, it is important to point

out that unless you have a means of cooking bread i.e. Dutch oven or solar oven, bread isn't going to be an option. You can substitute crackers for bread if needed. If you are planning on making the cornbread, you are going to need to have freeze-dried milk and eggs to complete the recipe.

That is just one example of a meal that is possible to prepare without electricity. As part of your prepping process, you will want to make sure and come up with ways of cooking and heating your meals.

Medium Term

Now it is time to start building up to six months of food on hand. Using the chilli example from above, you would need 48 cans of chilli. That is only a single night out of the week. One meal out of the 21 you will need to provide. Are you getting an image of the amount of space you will need?

Before we go any further with the food you need, we need to talk a bit about the space issue. A full, long-term food pantry is going to require a great deal of space. You will need a full closet, pantry or even a spare room to store all of your food. Shelving is a must. You absolutely don't want to put any food directly on the floor in case there is ever a flood, which can happen from a burst pipe or a busted water heater. Shelving should be sturdy enough to support a couple hundred cans of food.

You will also want to have a supply of food-grade buckets with lids on hand. These buckets are ideal for storing bulk items like grains, beans and pasta. Adding Mylar bags to your buckets is even better. You can find these in bulk online. Place your beans, flour, or whatever you are storing inside the bags. Seal the bags and place the bags inside the bucket. This will extend the shelf life of your dried food up to 15 years or more.

The space you choose for your prepper pantry should be somewhat dark. You don't want any direct sunlight streaming into the room. This will age your food and cause it to become stale and or possibly spoil. The space should also be dry. Basements are often used for food storage. This is a great way to utilize space in your home, but it is important there is plenty of ventilation to keep the area dry. Install a box fan or basement fan to help keep the air circulating.

Your food pantry will also need to be temperature controlled. You don't want the area to drop below 50 degrees Fahrenheit or go above 80 degrees. Another problem you want to avoid is pests. Pests can destroy a food pantry in a matter of days. It is crucial you monitor the area for intruders. Mice, ants, cockroaches, and anything else that poses a threat to your food supply needs to be taken care of immediately. If you need to hire a professional pest control service, do it! You can typically see signs of an invasion. At the first sign of trouble, set out traps, poison, or whatever is necessary to eliminate the problem. Take steps to prevent further invasions. A mouse only needs a hole the size of an American quarter to get in. Fill any holes or cracks in the wall with steel wool and caulking. This can also help block ants from making their way in.

Long Term

The golden number—one year of food on hand. This is something many preppers aspire to. It is a long road, but once you place that last can of green beans on the shelf, you will feel accomplished. You will have a sense that all will be okay no matter what comes your way. But, your journey doesn't end here. You will want to keep adding to your food pantry. Why? There are a couple of different reasons.

1-You can never have too much food on hand. If you have a lot, you are going to be sitting comfortably and will not have to worry as much when a late spring storm destroys your crops and limits the amount of food you can harvest. You will also have extra food that you can use to barter for other items you may not have. A healthy food supply also means you can share with those in need.

2-If you are up to a year's worth of food; it has probably taken you at least that long to build up the supply. That means you have some stuff that is getting old. You want to do your best to keep your food fresh. By rotating the old stuff out and replacing it with new, you will ensure your food is fresh when something does happen. A pantry full of expired or spoiled food is not going to do you a lot of good. You need to implement the first in, first out rule. Don't be afraid to add a new item to your pantry and pull out the oldest to serve for dinner.

The food you store in your pantry will depend on your family. You only store what your family eats today. Don't stock up on a bunch of canned spinach or canned sardines if your family doesn't eat them. They are not suddenly going to have a change of heart. Of course if they are truly starving they may choke it down, but they are not going to be happy about it.

It is just as important you diversify your food supply as well. You don't want to focus all of your energy into stocking 300 cans of chilli. Your tummy will not be happy. You and your family members can truly suffer from a condition known as food fatigue. Food fatigue happens when you eat the same food day in and day out for a long period of time. You need to shake things up a bit. The condition causes intestinal upset, meaning vomiting, diarrhoea, and stomach cramps. You cannot afford to get sick and possibly dehydrated when medical attention may not be readily available.

The following is a list of the foods you will want to add to your food storage. However, like it was mentioned earlier, skip an item if there is no way your family will eat it. Please note this list includes a lot of items for baking from scratch. You won't be able to run to the store for bread—you have to make it.

Grains
- Rice
- Flour
- Wheat
- Oats
- Granola
- Cornmeal

Beans
- Pinto
- Red
- Navy
- Kidney
- Lentils

Baking
- Baking powder
- Baking soda
- Cooking oil

- Shortening
- Sugar
- Salt
- Bouillon

Canned Meats
- Tuna
- Salmon
- Oysters
- Sardines
- Spam
- Corned beef
- Chicken

Canned Fruit and Veggies
- Corn, beans, peas
- Oranges, pears, peaches

Dried Foods
- Jerky
- Dried vegetables
- Dried fruit
- Dry soup

Miscellaneous
- Crackers
- Canned soup
- Coffee
- Tea
- Energy bars
- Chocolate
- Honey
- Canned chilli
- Freeze-dried dairy products; milk, cheese, butter

- Mac and Cheese
- Canned beans

If your children have a specific snack they really enjoy, do your best to stock up on it. You want to create as much of a normal atmosphere as possible. By giving your family some typical foods and meals, you will be adding a sense of normalcy to a time that is anything but.

Take advantage of sales and stock up when you see items on clearance. Instead of buying one box of mac and cheese when you go shopping, buy two. Put one in your everyday pantry and the other in your long term food storage pantry. This is one way to build up a little here and there without writing out one big check.

Chapter 2

Canning And Drying Your Fresh Food

You don't have to buy all of your canned food from the grocery store. In fact, you really don't want to. Canned food is notorious for being preserved with a high number of nitrates and/or sugar. At a time when water is going to be in short supply, you don't want to be eating foods that have high sodium content. You also don't want canned fruit that is soaking in sugar. It will wreak havoc on your teeth at a time when dentists are not going to be readily available.

There is supreme satisfaction in canning your own food fresh from the garden. It makes you feel as if you have accomplished something amazing and you have really. And, to be perfectly honest, it is a lot cheaper to can your own fruits and vegetables. You can even can your own meats.

Canning is only one of the ways you can preserve the excess from your garden. Drying or dehydrating fruits, vegetables, and meats is another option. Drying is a bit more time consuming, but it is much lighter and space friendly than canning. If you are storing food in your car or a bug out bag, dried food is always a better option than canned food.

Dried food can be eaten as is, think jerky or trail mix, or reconstituted to bring the food fairly close to its original state. One of the downsides to drying or dehydrating your food is the fact that you lose some of the nutritional value in the process. For fruits and veggies, the vitamins and minerals tend to be in the juice.

It is a good idea to learn how to do your own home canning and drying food so you can do it post-collapse. It is a skill you can pass down to your children as well. Fifty years ago, canning food was the norm in households. In the past couple of decades, we have gotten away from home preservation. The reasons why vary, but basically, we are too busy and would rather the convenience of commercially prepared foods over that effort it takes to take care of the job at home.

Pressure Canning

All vegetables and meat need to be canned with a pressure canner. A pressure cooker or pressure canner is a large pot that seals tight with a gauge on the top. A pressure cooker ensures food inside the jars is processed thoroughly. A simple pot of boiling water would not provide the same even cooking as a pressure cooker. Water boils at 212 degrees or thereabouts. It won't get any hotter. To kill the bacteria and enzymes in

If you are seeking to can a large quantity of food pressure canning is the best way to do it, Pressure cookers come in a wide range of styles and sizes to suit almost every budget and requirement.

meat and vegetables, you need a hotter temperature. A pressure canner at 15 psi, is processing the food at about 257 degrees Fahrenheit, therefore making it safe.

To can food at home, you will need a few supplies. You can buy these second hand or new.

- Pressure canner

- Jars—if buying used, inspect the jars thoroughly to check for cracks
- Lids and bands
- Canning tongs
- Strainer
- Funnel
- Pickling salt (optional)
- Pectin—for jams and jellies
- Vinegar--for pickling
- Labels or Sharpie for writing on lids
- A jar/can opener

Only use new lids for your canning. You absolutely do not want to risk ruining your food by using a contaminated lid or a lid that doesn't have the gummy substance to properly seal the jar. Bands can be reused; however, you need to check the bands thoroughly to make sure there is no rust. Rust on a band could ultimately contaminate your food.

Water Bath Canning

A large stock pot can be used to can fruits, jams, jellies, and apple sauce. Water bath canning is simply processing your fruits with boiling water. The boiling water is hot enough to kill off the enzymes in the fruit to make it safe for canning. To use the water bath canning method, you will want to put a wire rack on the bottom of your stock pot. This will prevent the jars from sitting directly on the bottom

If you are canning smaller quantities of food water bath canning is ideal as you can use the pots you have on hand with out having to resort to the expense of purchasing a pressure cooker

and getting too hot and cracking. When the water reaches the boiling point, carefully add the jars with jar tongs. You can buy a special wire rack that holds the jars in place so they do not bump each other during the boiling process. The water will need to be high enough to completely cover the jar. Process the jars for about 10 minutes or according to the guidelines of the recipe you are using.

Tips for Canning

- Use a damp towel to wipe off the edge of the jar before placing the lid on.
- After processing, screw the bands on. They will come loose during the canning process
- Once a lid is sealed, you can remove the bands from the jars and reuse them to can a new batch.
- Make sure the food is completely covered by liquid in the jars.
- When blanching vegetables, do not overcook the food. You want it to be slightly undercooked to retain crispness in the canning process. Typically, you will not boil vegetables for more than 5 minutes before placing them into jars for canning.

For drying and dehydrating, you have a couple of options. Dehydrating is the easiest and most common method of drying food at home. Drying is technically a process that relies on the sun and can take several days.

Dehydrating

- A quality dehydrator is crucial, size doesn't matter
- Lemon juice for preserving fruit
- Brine, seasoning for dehydrating meat

Drying

Sun-drying food is the most cost effective method for drying food, just make sure the food is screened off to prevent contamination by insects

Drying food outside is best done in a screened box designed for drying. The food will need to be placed on screens. It is also necessary to have a frame with a screen in it to keep bugs off your food. There are plans available for you to make one of these contraptions on the internet. Drying food with the sun will require high heat and unfiltered sun.

It is a good idea to have a combination of dried, canned, and freeze-dried foods. The latest will store for longer, but unfortunately, you cannot do that process at home. You can, however, successfully can and dry food that will sit on your shelf for years without spoiling.

It is important you follow the directions for canning. Don't try and cheat the system or cut corners. Doing so could risk the safety of the food. Vegetables and meat absolutely must be preserved in a pressure canner. Fruits are easier and can be processed in a boiling water bath or basically a stockpot on the stove.

Chapter 3

10 Easy And Delicious Recipes You Can Easily Prepare And Preserve

There are hundreds of different recipes you can employ to create tasty jars of canned food. Mixing fruit with sugar, lemon, or water is one option. Veggies canned with onions, garlic or plain salt will add more flavour and in some cases, a little more crunch to your vegetables. It is all personal preference.

Here are a few common recipes you can use to preserve the produce from your garden. Make sure you thoroughly wash all of your jars, lids and bands before you begin the canning process.

Recipes Which Can Be Canned

Light Strawberry Jam

- 4 cups crushed strawberries
- 1 cup unsweetened white grape juice
- 3 Tbsp Low or No-Sugar Needed Pectin

1. Combine strawberries and grape juice in a large pot.
2. Add in pectin and continue stirring the mixture over medium heat until a rolling boil is reached. The boil should be such that it doesn't disappear when you stir the mixture. Allow to boil for one minute.
3. Remove from heat and skim off the foam if desired. Use a ladle to fill 6 half-pint jars with the jam mixture.

4. Place a large stockpot filled with enough water to cover the jars with about ½ inch of water. Bring the water to a boil. Add the jars and process for 10 minutes. Remove the jars and set on a counter. The lids should pop or seal within 24 hours.

Stew Meat

- Meat—lamb, beef, pork, venison of your choice
- Water
- Canning salt
- Enough jars to hold meat

1. Cut meat into 1-inch cubes.
2. Remove as much fat and gristle as possible.
3. Place meat in a saucepan and cover with water. Allow the meat to cook until it is hot throughout. Use a meat thermometer to make sure it is all thoroughly heated. Remove the pan from heat.
4. Scoop the meat and water into jars making sure to leave at least a ¼ inch of head space at the top. Add a teaspoon of salt if desired.

5. Fill your pressure canner with enough water to cover the tops of the jars. Secure the lid on the canner and begin heating. You need to process the meat for 1 hour and 30 minutes at 10 pounds of pressure.

Chilli

- 4 lb boneless beef chuck
- 1/4 cup vegetable oil
- 3 cups diced onion (about 4 medium)
- 2 cloves garlic, minced

- 5 Tbsp chilli powder
- 2 tsp cumin seed
- 2 tsp salt
- 1 tsp oregano
- 1/2 tsp pepper
- 1/2 tsp coriander
- 1/2 tsp crushed red pepper
- 6 cups undrained and diced canned tomatoes

1. Cut meat into half inch cubes being careful to remove as much fat as possible.
2. Brown the meat over medium heat. Add in garlic and onions and cook until slightly transparent.
3. Add in remaining spices or season to taste and allow to cook for another five minutes.
4. Add in diced tomatoes, turn the heat to low and allow to simmer for 45 minutes.

5. Pour mixture into 3 quart jars or 6 pint jars. Process in pressure canner for 1 hour 30 minutes at 10 pounds of pressure.

Green Beans

- Green beans
- Water
- Salt (optional)

1. Wash beans and cut off ends.
2. Remove any obvious strings. Boil beans in water for about 5 minutes.
3. Pack beans into jars. Add ½ teaspoon of salt if desired. Pour boiling water over the top, leaving ¼ inch head space.

4. Process beans at 10 pounds for 20 minutes.

Bread and Butter Pickles

- 3 1/2 lbs pickling cucumbers (about 14 small to medium)
- 2 1/2 cups vinegar (5% acidity)
- 2 1/2 cups sugar
- 1/4 cup Bread & Butter Pickle Mix

1. Wash cucumbers and cut off the ends.
2. Slice the cucumbers into half-inch slices.
3. In a small saucepan, heat vinegar, sugar, and pickle seasoning mix. Pack cucumber slices into jar.
4. Pour boiling spice mixture over the top. Process in boiling water bath for 15 minutes.

5. Allow pickles to ferment for at least 4 weeks before opening.

Recipes You Can Dehydrate

Peaches and Pears

- 1 cup peaches
- ½ cup pears

1. Peel peaches and pears and slice into strips.
2. Place fruit on a special sheet for using in your dehydrator.

3. Dehydrate fruit until it becomes leathery.

Granola

You will need a variety of dried fruits for this recipe. If you haven't dried them yet, you can buy them in the grocery store.

- 4 cups Rolled old fashion oats
- 1/2 cup Chopped pecans
- 1/2 cup Raisins
- 1/2 cup Dried pineapple
- 1/2 cup Craisins
- 1/2 cup Walnuts
- 1/2 cup Chopped dried apples
- 1/2 cup Chopped dried apple peels
- 1/2 cup Chopped dried bananas
- 1/2 cup Olive oil
- 1/2 cup Honey
- 1/2 tsp Vanilla

1. In a small saucepan, heat the olive oil, honey, and vanilla together.
2. Place the dry ingredients in a bowl and drizzle the wet mixture over the top.
3. Mix together to coat all of the ingredients. Pour the mixture into a fruit leather pan and place in dehydrator at 125 degrees.

4. Let the mixture dry until desired.

Maple Jerky

- 1 pound meat of your choice, thinly sliced
- 2 tablespoons Dijon mustard
- 2 tablespoons pure maple syrup

- ½ teaspoon salt

1. In a small bowl, combine mustard, salt, and syrup. Add in meat strips to coat thoroughly.
2. Place meat in refrigerator for several hours to allow it to marinate.
3. Cook meat in a 350 degree oven for about 10 minutes or until meat is no longer pink. Place meat strips on dehydrator rack.

4. Dehydrate for 8 hours or until meat is dry.

Dehydrated Milk

- ½ gallon 1 percent milk

1. Place parchment paper on the fruit leather tray of your dehydrator making sure to create an edge by wrapping the paper around the upper lip of the tray.
2. Pour the milk onto the paper being careful not to overflow the lining. Dehydrate for 10 hours at 135 degrees.

3. When milk is dry, put the mixture into a blender and pulse until a fine powder.

Jalapeno Powder

- Fresh jalapeños from the garden

Wash the jalapeños and cut off the stems. Cut the peppers in half and remove the seeds. Place peppers on the dehydrator trays and allow to dry for a full 24 hours at 90 degrees. Place dried peppers in a blender and mix until a fine powder is formed.

Chapter 4

How To Efficiently And Safely Store Water

Water is an absolute necessity. You need to store enough water to keep your family alive. One gallon of water per day per person is the minimum amount of water you need. A typical family of four would need about 30 gallons for a single week. A case of bottled water is just under 1.5 gallons of water, which is about 15 cases for a week. Now you can probably see why you need to come up with an efficient way to store your water. It takes up a great deal of space and it is very heavy.

You probably do not have enough room in your house to store that much water. You need options. One of the things many preppers get hung up on is the idea they need to store enough drinkable water for a year. You don't. Yes, you will want to store some water that can be consumed without treating it, but you don't need to have 300 gallons of potable water on hand.

As long as you have water on hand, you can treat it to make it safe to drink as long as you plan ahead. You can store household bleach, purification tablets, or a portable filter. You can also boil the water to make it safe to drink. No matter which method you choose, you need to have a way to purify the water to remove viruses and bacteria.

Boiling your water is one of easiest ways to kill microbes in your water but in an emergency situation this may consume valuable energy.

If you live near a lake, river, or other body of water, you can get away with storing less water.

Storing Water

You will want to think big when it comes to storing water. Rain barrels are an excellent option. They won't take up room inside your house and each barrel can hold more then 50 gallons of water. The barrels can be stored in a shed, garage, or

Rain water barrels are one of the easiest and most affordable ways to recycle and store pure rain water

outside against a north-facing wall. You can opt to use a garden hose to fill the barrels or let the rain do the work. Place empty barrels under a corner of the roof to catch the most water. You can also use a down spout to direct the water into the barrel.

If you have the space, you can use stackable water containers stored inside your garage or an out building. The containers each have handles and spouts and tend to hold anywhere from 3 to 5 gallons. The containers are square and have grooves that allow them to form a wall when stacked. You can cover the containers with a tarp or blanket to help shield them from the sun and excessive heat.

Dark coloured containers are best and will help block the sunlight. Never use containers that have held dangerous chemicals. The chemicals are absorbed in the plastic. When the plastic of the container is heated, the chemicals will leech into your water supply.

You can store water at home in various containers to help save money. It is never a good idea to use old milk jugs to store water. The jugs are made of a flimsy plastic that will break down within a matter of months. You can fill old soda and juice bottles. The heavier plastic will hold up for years. Add a drop of bleach to your home-bottled water and date the container for six months. The water is safe to drink within that time period. If it has been more than six months, you can treat the water and make it safe once again.

Swimming pools, hot tubs, and backyard ponds are also water storage options. However, this water will need to be treated before drinking. Wait to use water from a swimming pool or hot tub for several days after the power has gone out. This allows the chemicals used in the pools to dissipate and evaporate.

Do your best to maximize every inch of space in your home. Remove the small bottles of water that are sold by the case and stack them under your bed. The 2-liter soda bottles can also be stored under your bed or under the bathroom sink. Do your best to find space inside your home where the temperature is regulated and you can limit sun exposure.

If you live on your own land, you can invest in large cisterns that are buried underground. It is best to have these buried on a hill to take advantage of gravity. However, if a hill isn't available, you can use a hand pump to get the water out of the cistern. If you have your own well, make sure you have a hand pump ready to use if the power goes out.

Chapter 5

How To Manage Your Food And Water Properly If There Is An Emergency

When an emergency strikes, you need to implement a plan that will stretch your supplies. You don't want to go on a binge and eat all of your canned food simply because it is there. You need to ration your food and water. It may look like a lot, but if you have no idea how long you will be forced to make do on your own, you can't afford to burn through your supplies within the first week.

Two important rules you must get across to your family are you don't eat until you are full and you don't eat because you are bored. It is absolutely important the family understands the food is there to help you survive, not to provide comfort or something to do.

You can help prevent the rush on your food supply by taking some time today to plan a menu of sorts that you will use when it is time to rely on your food storage. Your menu planning should be based on caloric content, not on how much it takes to feel full. Check out the following chart to determine how many calories each member of your family should be getting each day.

*An average male will need about 2,500 to 2,800 calories per day. Older males are on the lower end of the scale.

*An average female will need about 1,800 to 2,100 calories per day.

*Children will need about 1,400 calories per day. Younger

children will need less.

These calorie guidelines are based on a semi-active lifestyle. If you are going to be doing strenuous labour, you would need more calories to replace what you burn. Likewise, if you are more sedentary, then you will have food left over. That does not mean it should be consumed right away but rather it should be saved.

It is more important than ever that you read the labels on any commercially packaged food. You are not eating solely for the joy and satisfaction of eating. You are doing so to stay alive. You need to check the contents of your canned or freeze- dried food. You don't want to go overboard on salt, sugar or even meat. You need to be able to create as close to a balanced meal as possible. Veggies, fruits, meat, and pasta will all help keep you going and healthy.

Water is going to be extremely important. Technically you only need a gallon a day, but if it is hot and you are doing manual labour, you will need more water in order to stay hydrated. You can help avoid dehydration by resting during the heat of the day and doing your chores in the cooler evening and early morning hours.

Having bottled water on hand is nice simply because it is a little easier to ration. Each person gets a bottle of water to last them for a few hours. The idea is to stay hydrated, which only requires a few sips here and there.

Teach kids how to brush their teeth and wash their hands with as little water as possible. Sponge bathing will also help conserve water. To wash dishes, you need to use potable water to avoid contaminating your clean dishes with water that contains bacteria and viruses. If you haven't stored paper plates and disposable cutlery, you need to plan on additional water to take care of cleaning needs.

Do your best to include some snacks in your daily rations. This will help you and your kids to feel normal and can help stave off hunger. If you allow yourself to become hungry, you are more likely to gorge and eat far more than you truly need. Plan ahead and set aside meals for the day when possible.

Limit freeze-dried foods to once per day if possible to conserve water. Fortunately, most freeze-dried foods need little water to be transformed into delicious meals. However, you need to factor the water needed for those meals into your daily usage. Dehydrated foods will take much more water to reconstitute. Eat dehydrated foods as is or put them in stews or soups that will allow you to conserve water while slowly reconstituting the food.

Chapter 6

The Best Ways to Scavenge and Restock Your Supplies

If your supplies are running low or you didn't plan a long enough food storage plan; you are going to need to scavenge for food and other supplies. This can be a bit difficult if you are not accustomed to taking things that are not yours. You have to put yourself into the mind-set that everybody is fighting to survive. Looting and scavenging are not the same. Looting would be stealing televisions, Xboxs, and things that are valuable, but hold no real value in a post-apocalyptic world. Taking things with the intent of selling it to get rich is looting. Scavenging food, diapers, toilet paper and soap is necessary and is almost a given. That will be a way of life.

The owners of the local store are already counting their inventory as a total loss. This would only be the case if you were dealing with something devastating like an act of war or a power grid failure that turned the world upside down. Scavenging when people are still trying to make a go out of their business is wrong and you don't want to do it.

You may also need to scavenge your neighbours' homes. If you know for certain neighbours have bailed out or have been killed, scavenging is a little easier to accept. Never try to take food and supplies from another family. It is wrong and it only incites trouble. You would be putting yourself at risk by trying to take something from others who are willing to fight to the death to keep it.

Scavenging is dangerous. It will require you to visit areas that are populated. You won't be the only one scavenging. Folks who are starving, freezing, or dying of thirst are going to be at the same super center searching for any scrap they can find.

It is best if you go on scavenging missions at a time when most people will be asleep. Early morning hours, between 3 and 5am, are a good time. Yes, it will be dark, but the darkness will provide you cover. The only people who should go on these scavenging missions are those who are in good physical health and can run and carry heavy loads. Children do not make good scavengers. When possible, assemble 3-man teams to scavenge. This will make sure there is somebody to keep a lookout while you are gathering supplies. It also allows you to get more supplies on a single run.

Highways are generally a good place to scavenge. Abandoned cars will likely hold plenty of booty. You may be able to siphon gas from the cars stranded on the road to get enough fuel to get you to a more rural location.

Bartering is one of the more ideal options. It is lawful and you won't have to worry about hurting somebody else. It is almost a given you are going to want or need something after the world suffers a chaotic event. In order to get what you need, prepare to barter for it. Bartering some of your home-canned food, your stash of chocolate or even a few rolls of toilet paper can get you things you need to survive.

Bartering items are going to be things that are cheap and plentiful in today's world. Things that we have come to love and may have some strong addictions to, like tobacco or chocolate, are going to be in high demand. You can prepare to barter by stocking up on these items. Bartering for fuel for your generator or medical services is going to be the new norm. Money will likely be worthless so you need to be able to barter with the supplies you have on hand.

Scavenging will also include searching for food in the wild. Hunting animals and foraging from plants and wild growing berries will also be a necessity. This is one way to restock your dwindling supplies. It is a good idea to forage and hunt when items are plentiful. It won't be long until wild animals are depleted and the plants are all picked. Take the time to start a garden or build a greenhouse so you have your own supply of food. Fresh fruits and veggies will also make excellent bartering tools.

Do your best to avoid the need to scavenge. It is risky business that will likely end in some kind of trouble. When you do head back to your home or wherever it is you are hunkering down, pay close attention to your surroundings and make sure you are not followed.

Conclusion

Taking the time and energy to plan an adequate food and water storage can save you a great deal of trouble, and even your life, in the event disaster strikes. We never know when a natural disaster, act of war, or a government collapse will send the world as we know it into a tailspin. We have to be prepared to survive on our own without the luxury or convenience of grocery stores or government aid.

If a disaster is significant enough, your family could be left fending for themselves for weeks, months, or possibly years. You simply can't leave it to chance. You need to take your life into your own hands and start putting away food and water that will keep you going in the immediate aftermath of a chaotic event. Make plans to grow a garden and become familiar with hunting. Your food and water will only last so long. You have to be prepared to find more food and water.

Good luck to you and just remember that slow and steady will always win the race. You don't have to buy a year's worth of food today. Set goals and build up your food supply over a period of time.

From The Author

Thank you for reading this book. As an author, I understand the importance of creating books which my readers will find both enjoyable and informative. If you have the time and feel generous, please leave an honest review of this book..........Steve Plant

No...I insist...Thank You!

www.ingramcontent.com/pod-product-compliance
Lightning Source LLC
Chambersburg PA
CBHW060444290526
45793CB00002B/568